Introducing
BEN NEVIS

The Mountain

Ben Nevis from Corpach c.1830.

INTRODUCING BEN NEVIS
The Mountain

BEN NEVIS, or the Ben as it is fondly known locally, sits majestically at the head of Loch Linnhe, its presence dominating the landscape from all corners of Lochaber.

The dramatic effect of the Ben, Britain's highest mountain, is emphasised by the fact that it begins its rise from the shores of Loch Linnhe, to tower 4,406ft (1,344m) above the town of Fort William, providing an almost paternal presence.

But what does "Nevis" mean? The river and glen running past the mountain both carry the name, as does the remote sea loch at Knoydart, 40 miles to the west. In gaelic the mountain's name, Beinn Nimheis, has been linked with Irish and gaelic words meaning poisonous or terrible, implying a fairly ominous character.

The nature of the Ben can indeed be changeable. While there may be a welcoming sea breeze on the shores of Loch Linnhe, 20-30 knots of chilling wind may be evident on the summit of the Ben. And many walkers/climbers find weather conditions changing within minutes – usually for the worse – as they toil their way up her flanks. Those heading for a stroll up the path should be warned that the Ben can be intolerant of the inexperienced, ill-prepared walker!

To the south and east, the Ben borders on the splendours of Glen Nevis. Here, perfectly u-shaped valleys, great waterfalls, hanging valleys and corries are a reminder of the tremendous geological activity which took place millions of years ago. The ancient Caledonian Mountain Range, of which Ben Nevis was a part, once stretched from Scandinavia to the Eastern side of North America. Formed 500 million years ago, this massive granite range became fragmented as the continents divided.

Shortly after, (in geological terms) the northern part of the Caledonian mountains in Scotland "slid" more than 60 miles southward and the Great Glen was formed.

Finally, as the last ice age retreated 10,000 years ago, Ben Nevis and her sister mountains were revealed, as enormous glaciers met the advance of the more temperate southern climate.

Industry

The British Aluminium Company opened its first smelter on the shores of Loch Ness in 1896, and over the next 33 years work took place on a remarkable hydro-electric scheme culminating in the opening of the Fort William smelter in 1929. The company's factory, built at the foot of Ben Nevis, harnesses the hydropower from Loch Treig and Loch Laggan through a tunnel fifteen miles long and fifteen feet in diameter. In this major

feat of engineering, all streams and rivers from Ben Nevis are also fed into the scheme, and the water is then channelled into the power house through five pipes visible on the northern flank of Meall an t-Suidhe.

The greatest annual rainfall of 240 inches was recorded at the Ben Nevis Observatory in 1898. Assuming that one inch of rain equates to approximately 100 tons of water per acre, and Ben Nevis summit covers almost 10 acres, it is hardly surprising that the British Aluminium Company sought to take advantage of the quarter of a million tons of water cascading down the Ben each year.

Alcan, Primary and Recycling, as the company is now known, is the owner of Ben Nevis up to the 2,500ft contour line, and leases the remainder of the mountain from the Fairfax Lucy Trustees. The company presently produces 50,000 tonnes of aluminium each year from its Lochaber smelters at Kinlochleven and Fort William.

The north face of the mountain through frosted birches at Muirshearlich.

Opposite page: *A ray of sunshine breaks though the clouds during a heavy shower over Ben Nevis.*

Fort William's only distillery still in production is well worth a visit.

Dew of Ben Nevis

The Ben Nevis Distillery has been producing quality whiskies at the foot of Britain's highest mountain since 1825, when John MacDonald of Keppoch first established the company. He was a giant of a man in every way, and the blend he produced was called Long John's Dew of Ben Nevis. Today the distillery which is one of Scotland's oldest, produces a variety of blended and single malts. The recently opened visitor centre offers guided tours of the age-old process of instilling 'life' into the abundant waters of Ben Nevis!

Opposite page:
The clear mountain waters of the Allt á Mhuilinn burn which flows down the Ben to the Ben Nevis Distillery at Lochy Bridge.

First Climbs

There is no record of when Ben Nevis was first climbed, although ascents, presumably by the same general line as the present tourist path, were certainly being made by the early part of the 18th century. By the 19th century it was becoming fashionable to include an ascent of Ben Nevis in a grand tour of Scotland. The poet John Keats for example, made an ascent with Charles Brown and a local guide in August 1818, which inspired him to write a sonnet at the summit.

The footpath just above Achintee in Glen Nevis was originally constructed in the summer of 1883 by the Scottish Meteorological Society.

The path is easily seen on the side of Meall an t-Suidhe, in Glen Nevis, locally pronounced Melan T. A trail leading up from the Youth Hostel joins the main path.

Opposite page:
The water of the River Nevis is supplied by tributaries from the surrounding Mamore mountains and, of course, Ben Nevis.

Upper Glen Nevis and the treacherous water slide of Allt Coire Eòghainn on the southern side of Ben Nevis.

In May 1880 William Naismith and two clerical friends travelled down the Caledonian Canal by steamer, and then made headlines in the national press by making the first ascent of Ben Nevis without a guide. Nine years later Naismith instigated the formation of the Scottish Mountaineering Club, and in 1892 he formulated 'Naismith's Rule' which is still used today to estimate the time required for outings in the mountains.

One of the first routes pioneered on the precipitous north face of Ben Nevis was

As the clouds clear from a snow covered Ben Nevis, a solitary Scots pine stands exposed in Glen Nevis.

Opposite page:
Highland cattle enjoy the sunshine in Glen Nevis.

The old observatory ruin and summit cairn from the west.

Mr Bert Bissell from Dudley first climbed Ben Nevis in 1938 and inaugurated the Peace Cairn in 1945. Since then, and pictured here at the age of 90, Bert has climbed to the summit 107 times. He is the oldest person to have made as many ascents. He died in November 1998 and was buried in Glen Nevis Cemetery.

probably a snow and ice climb now known as Number 3 Gully.

An early winter ascent was witnessed by a member of staff at the new Observatory shortly after it opened in the mid-1880's.

The first rock climb recorded on Ben Nevis was made in September 1892 by the Hopkinson family from Lancashire. Their audacious attempt on the huge central ridge on the north face failed the first day high up on the mountain, but the following day the three brothers, John, Albert and Charles, together with John's son Bertram, descended from the summit plateau and crossed an exciting gap to gain the summit of a prominent feature now known as the Great Tower. They then descended the steep west face of the Tower to reach their previous high point.

Opposite page:
Ben Nevis summit from the air.

From here they retraced their steps down the ridge.

Tower Ridge, the finest ridge on the mountain, had been conquered – albeit from the top.

The Ben Nevis Observatory

The Ben Nevis Observatory was opened on the 17th October 1883, and for the next 20 years meteorological data was gathered on an hourly basis from the highest observatory in Britain. The observatory had two main aims; firstly to give warnings of approaching Atlantic storms which influence European weather, and secondly to take advantage of the sea-level observatory in Fort William, to investigate vertical gradients of pressure, temperature and humidity.

Prior to the formal scientific readings being undertaken, a remarkable personality, Clement L. Wragge, climbed the Ben every day during the summer of 1881 to make observations. This rather eccentric gentleman, who became known locally as "Inclement Wragge," was

The impressive north face of Ben Nevis with Loch Linnhe far below. The mountain provides some of the most demanding ice climbs in Europe.

The summit shelter and Observatory ruins in June 1987.

Opposite page:
Sunrise on Ben Nevis summit above Gardyloo Gully.

awarded the Meteorological Society's gold medal for his work, and subsequently became Government Meteorologist in Queensland, where he established the weather Bureau at Brisbane, and mountain observatories on Mount Wellington and Koshiusho.

The observatory was built mainly from private donations, and Queen Victoria headed the subscription list. The sum of £4,000 was raised within a few months, and the path to the summit and the observatory building were constructed five months later. The observatory's designer was T. Stevenson (father of writer Robert Louis) who was well respected as a lighthouse engineer and designer of the thermometer screen.

A committee comprising members of the Scottish Meteorological Society and representatives nominated by

the Royal Societies of London and Edinburgh, managed the observatory, and the building was generally manned by the Superintendent and two assistants. These were the men who battled against ferocious gales to obtain their hourly readings. From November until May the observatory building was covered by snow, and the men had to tunnel through 30ft drifts to reach the outside world. In winter and spring, when the summit was often enveloped in cloud for long periods, and the temperature was below freezing point, the super-cooled cloud droplets froze on coming into contact with any object on the mountain top.

An unusual view of the mountain from Blarmafoldach in the west.

For 170 years shipping has passed through the Caledonian Canal with Ben Nevis towering above.

Ben Nevis and Fort William from the Ardgour side of Loch Linnhe.

Opposite page: *Regardless of time of year Ben Nevis can be relied upon to provide a picture – this one was taken on the shore of Loch Linnhe, adjacent to the Caledonian Canal and is in contrast to the one featured over the centre spread pages which was taken from the canal itself.*

In strong winds, this deposit was severe, and it was occasionally impossible for even a roped observer to reach the Stevenson screen.

To enable the management committee to examine vertical variations of the physical properties of the atmosphere, a further observatory was established at sea level in Fort William, and the schoolmaster took readings five times daily to compare with those on the mountain summit. During the observatory's life it was calculated that the average rainfall on the summit was four metres compared to two metres in Fort William, and the mean annual temperature was just below freezing on the summit, and generally 9°C lower than in Fort William.

There was no shortage of volunteers to relieve the full-time observers during the summer months, but winters were a long tour of duty. Nine months food supply had to be stored on the summit, as ponies were unable to make the rigorous journey.

Opposite page:
The Ben Nevis Observatory, mostly covered in snow, operated from 1883-1904.

Hotel staff at the natural spring near the top of the mountain.

Provisions were taken to the summit by pony whenever the weather allowed.

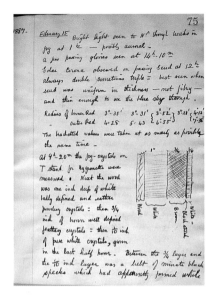

A half way station also recorded weather details. In these photographs, taken by Alexander Drysdale, a former observer, staff take time out for the camera and this chap obviously looked forward to his morning wash 'al fresco'.

Inside the office of the Ben Nevis Observatory. Two observers and a cook lived on the mountain sometimes for up to three months at a time.

Opposite page:
Careful teamwork by observers on the summit c.1890 above Gardyloo Gully. Below them 2,000 feet of rockface and lots of fresh air!

The observers kept themselves amused during their free time; their main pursuit being tobogganing. It seems amazing that despite the gradients there were very few accidents, although one observer had a near miss when he attached sails to his sled and nearly accompanied it over a precipice!

The observatory drew the presence of many eminent people of the time, including Captain Scott, who was given permission to test some of his Antarctic equipment on the summit prior to his famous expedition. Unable to attend himself, a Lieutenant Royds took his place. An entrepreneurial Fort William hotelier established an annex on the summit which provided a fascinating residence for the adventurous traveller.

During its twenty years of operation, the majority of the funding for the observatory came from private donations, and the extensive findings were published in four volumes by the Royal Society of Edinburgh. However, it became obvious that without the assurance of state support, the observatory would have to cease operating. Sadly, this financial assistance, which would have amounted to £950 annually, was not forthcoming, and the last readings were taken on 1st October 1904.

During 1983 celebrations were held to mark the centenary of the observatory. Activities included a trip to the summit by pony, BMX bike and Landrover! A camp was also established on the summit and weather reports were transmitted to Aviemore Met Office.

TRANSPORT

On 6th October 1928, George Simpson of Edinburgh succeeded in taking a Baby Austin motorcar to the summit. At one point on the journey, the car was precariously balanced over a precipice after chains being used to prevent the wheels slipping, snapped. The ascent took 7 hours 23 minutes and was entered in the Guiness Book of Records. The descent at less than 2 hours was apparently equally tricky! The photograph above of the Austin on the Ben, was taken by John Nelson, also of Edinburgh, who was employed in Fort William at the time on the construction of the Smelter and Inverlochy village. Earlier efforts in 1911 saw Henry Alexander succeeding in getting a model T Ford to the summit.

Opposite page:
The summit cairn and shelter enveloped in winter's firm grip.

The Ben Nevis Race

The Ben Nevis Race began in 1895 on a rather informal basis when William Swan ran from the old Post Office in Fort William to the summit of the Ben and back in 2 hours 41 minutes. Having thrown down this gauntlet, the competition commenced, and continued until the Observatory closed in 1904.

After a thirty year break, the race was reintroduced in 1937. With interruptions during and after the second world war, it has been run annually since 1951.

Now, each year on the first Saturday in September, this international event attracts many more than the 200 official entries, and is organised by a 16 man committee assisted by the police and forces. Bearing in mind that the average, fit person will reach the summit and return to sea-level in 5-6 hours, race times are staggering. The present record is held by Ken Stuart of Keswick who completed the course in 1 hour, 25 minutes and 33 seconds in 1984.

An earlier race start from times gone by (c.1900).

Opposite page:
Competitors in the annual Ben Nevis Race ascend via the footpath.

On the summit plateau but not quite there – still a bit to go...

The current rescue team. (1993)

A Sea King helicopter from Lossiemouth rescues an injured climber from Observatory Ridge.

CIC – Charles Ingles Clark memorial hut belonging to the Scottish Mountaineering Club is used as a base whilst climbing on Ben Nevis. In the background Carn Dearg Buttress where some of the longest and hardest climbs are found.

Lochaber Mountain Rescue Team

Until 1970, the mountain rescue team was a section of the local mountaineering club, and was the first civilian team in Scotland. During 1970, the group was formally constituted, and is now one of the top three mountain rescue teams in the country. It is also one of the busiest with an average of 60 call-outs each year, most of which are to Ben Nevis to assist hillwalkers.

The team is made up of 35 experienced mountaineers, who all offer their services voluntarily. They work closely with the RAF Search and Rescue Services, whose helicopters are critical in ensuring that casualties receive speedy attention. The local police in Fort William are also a vital link in the rescue chain. It is they who call out the team, and who provide necessary insurance cover and some financial support.

Nevis Garage assists the team by helping to provide special 4-wheel drive Volkswagon vehicles which allow a search party or rescue unit and all their equipment to reach the scene of an accident without delay.

Opposite page:
Air sea rescue helicopter is called in to assist Lochaber Mountain Rescue team evacuate a casualty from the mountain.

On the last few feet of Tower Ridge climb with Loch Eil far below.

Approaching the summit of Carn Mór Dearg with NE Buttress and Ben Nevis summit on the right. The hills of Glencoe in the background.

The Glen Nevis River Race

This annual race is the main fund raising event for Lochaber Mountain Rescue Team. The first race was held in 1969, and it has been an attraction in Glen Nevis since then. In August 1992 the event raised almost £6,000. The course is approximately 1.5 miles down the river and over the lower falls on an airbed – and yes, the water is cold! Around 150 competitors are expected each year and everyone, particularly the spectators have a great afternoon.

Opposite page:
Looking along the cliffs to Carn Dearg NE from the summit plateau of Ben Nevis.

Three faces of Ben Nevis. The towering cliffs of the mountain are locked in ice and snow for several months of the year. Even in late August snow persists in crevasses where sunshine seldom reaches.

Opposite page:
Ben Nevis viewed from a heatherfield on the Blar, a peat bog which lies adjacent to the West Highland Line near Banavie.

Ben Nevis massif in summer colours from Loch Eil-side.

Nature

Despite the inhospitable nature of the mountain, a surprising variety of wild flowers, heathers and mosses grow quite happily in many areas.

Several species of saxifrage can be seen beside the footpath, and in late July water lobelia provide a beautiful pale blue blanket over the surface of the lochan.

Here, you may occasionally

Opposite page:
Low cloud clears from the mountain in the evening sunshine. This view is from Torlundy forest.

see heron feeding, and the common sandpiper is a summer visitor. Ravens take advantage of air currents round the cliffs, and although golden eagles are shy, you may see one soaring above the Mamores or the Grey Corries.

The Ben provides a breeding ground for frogs and newts, and its heathers house cocoons of moths. Her north facing corries experience the most severe weather in Britain, and support some of the hardiest and rare plant species. And there are always the intrepid wanderers – one group of mountaineers came across a badger on the north east face!

Ben Nevis attracts many thousand visitors each year. For some, it is the thrill and excitement associated with mastering her northern face, others walk up her flanks for charity, exercise or fun, many just come to gaze ...

The Ben is an important part of our heritage to be enjoyed and savoured, and to be treated with respect and care.

Gaelic Terms
Nimheis (Nevis): **Poison**
Lochan Meall an t'Suidhe:
Small loch of the Hill of the Seat
Polldubh: **Black pool**
Achadh an t'Suidhe (Achintee):
Field of the Seat
Ach nan Cu: **Field of the Dogs**
Allt à Mhuilinn: **Stream of the mill**
An Steal: **the Spout**
Meall an t'Suidhe: **Hill of the Seat**

Further Reading
Twenty Years on Ben Nevis
by Wm T. Kilgour

*Ben Nevis Observatory
1883-1904*
Royal Meteorological Society

Ben Nevis
Ken Crocket

Overleaf:
The Allt á Mhuilinn burn pours down from Britain's highest mountain as the weather suddenly clears.
Back cover:
Ben Nevis in mid summer from Tomacharich.